What the heck should I do?

What the heck should I do?

YOUR STEP-BY-STEP GUIDE
TO MAKING THE RIGHT ACADEMIC
AND CAREER CHOICES

Ariane Masson

Cover and illustrations: Lucie

ISBN: 9798736728992

Success is not the key to happiness.
Happiness is the key to success.
If you love what you are doing, you will be successful.

— Albert Schweitzer

The same wind blows on us all;
the winds of disaster, opportunity and change.
Therefore, it is not the blowing of the wind,
but the setting of the sails
that will determine our direction in life.

— Jim Rohn

TABLE OF CONTENTS

Introduction

Welcome to one of the most inspiring journeys of your life, the journey towards a meaningful and successful career!

I designed this guide to support you in navigating the overwhelming process of choosing a career and the academic or training path that goes with it.

What is a career? It's a journey which includes education, training, and work experience in one occupation, or a series of related occupations.

Choosing a career is a big deal. Why? Because your career choice will greatly influence how you spend your time, how much money you have, what people you meet, where you live. It will even contribute to the meaning you give to your life.

Career planning should be inspiring and exciting. It can be a deeply enriching experience, but most often it is a source of anxiety and indecision. The risk is then to make the default choice, the one that pleases others, the one that is the most prestigious, or the one that seems the easiest. Choosing the wrong path is most often synonymous with lack of motivation and academic failure. Later, it makes it more difficult to find meaningful employment. Did you know that only 13% of workers worldwide actually enjoy their jobs? You don't have to join the ranks of people who are unhappy with their work.

This book draws on the work and experience of psychologists and guidance professionals. Its aim is to help you build your career path step by step. It provides you with the right questions to ask yourself so as to determine your professional identity. It then helps you explore the professional world to target careers in which you can succeed. It also guides you in finding the relevant educational or training path.

This book is for you if you're facing the following transitions:

You're a high school student wondering what courses to take and what to do after high school.

You're starting college and have to decide what to study or what majors to choose.

You've just graduated and are about to begin your job search.

You're already in the workforce and looking to switch jobs or change careers.

You're a parent and want to help your children with their academic and career choices.

You're a guidance counselor looking for effective tools.

This book will not make the decision for you but guide you in your reflection and research. Only you can decide your professional future. For this, you must be ready to give yourself time to reflect on yourself and do some thorough research.

For more information, please visit our companion website www.whattheheckshouldIdo.com.

The 6 traps to avoid

Before you start your journey, let me warn you of the most common pitfalls you may encounter on your way.

Trap #1: Choosing your academic or training path without a career plan

A common mistake is to postpone choices to keep your options open. You don't know what kind of career you want. Hence, you keep your educational goals broad. But by not making them more specific, you may be closing doors. For instance, if you haven't taken the necessary courses in physics at undergraduate level, it will be next to impossible to pursue graduate studies in physics.

Your career plan should dictate your academic or training path, not the other way around. Else you may waste a lot of time and money for diplomas or certifications that will be of no use. In addition, it is much more exciting to study or train with a career goal in mind.

Trap #2: No taking the time to get to know yourself well

Some people go through life without knowing who they are and what they really want out of life. To choose a career, you need to know your values, aptitudes, and aspirations.

Trap #3: Leaving the decision to someone else

You may be tempted to trust the advice of people around you: your parents, your friends, or your teachers. You may also be influenced by what's trending right now, the most popular career paths. Yet who better than yourself can know what you want? It's your life. Follow your own script! Don't choose a career just because someone else thinks it's a good idea. This book is here to help you arrive at your own decision.

Trap #4: Relying solely on your academic results to make a choice

Your personality is not limited to your report card. Resist the temptation to consider only those subjects you're good at when choosing your academic or training path. Conversely, don't rule out an entire career field because you struggle in a specific subject: if you find meaning in what you're doing, you will overcome most learning difficulties with hard work. Finally, keep in mind that loving a subject does not mean that you can easily turn it into a career. For instance, you may appreciate literature; this does not mean that you will make a good English teacher. Check that you want to teach!

Trap #5: Choosing alone

It's the opposite of trap #3. Once your personal reflection is well under way, it is crucial that you talk with the relevant people to get feedback on your career plans. We will come back to this.

Trap #6: Limiting the range of possibilities

Like most people, you certainly have your share of beliefs about what careers are available to you because of your gender, social background, heredity, or geographic location. At this stage, it is essential that you widen your horizons.

Your journal

Choose an environment conducive to focus and introspection. Please plan to allow at least 2 hours to complete the questionnaires.

Get hold of a notebook and a pencil or pen. You will use them every time you see the following image:

Your notebook will serve as a journal to build your career plan. In it, you will record your answers to the questionnaires and research careers and educational institutions.

Throughout your journey, take the time to write down what spontaneously comes to mind, including questions and topics you want to explore. Don't censor yourself! Journaling stimulates creativity and helps resolve inner conflicts. No one needs to see this notebook but yourself.

Ready to plan your career?

Reconnect!

Career planning starts with knowing yourself well.

In the next chapter, you will take the RIASEC questionnaire, which comprises a series of 26 multiple-choice questions to uncover your preferences, personality traits, and skills.

Before taking this questionnaire, I invite you to do a little introspection exercise to reconnect with your inner self. Indeed, social and family pressures often make us lose sight of our true aspirations. We want to convey a certain image; we put on a social mask which eventually merges with who we think we are. It is therefore useful to take the time to reconnect with yourself before taking the RIASEC questionnaire.

Answer the **15 questions below** in your notebook. Again, don't censor yourself and write down everything that spontaneously comes to mind.

1. What did you dream of doing when you were a child?

✎ ......

2. What career would you choose if everything were possible, and you didn't care what others thought of you?

To answer this question, imagine there are no obstacles, either financial or in terms of skills. Visualize yourself doing your dream job.

✎ ....

3. You have just turned 70 and your professional career is behind you. What do you absolutely want to have achieved?

✎ ....

4. Are you ready to choose a career? What's standing in your way?

Beliefs, lack of self-confidence, a sense of duty

✎ ....

5. What keeps you from being yourself?

✎ ....

6. Do you care what your parents think? Your friends? When do you care?

✎ ....

7. Which traits of your personality do you value most? Why?

✎ ....

8. Which traits of your personality do you dislike most? Why?

✎ ....

9. What experiences had the greatest impact on you?

✎ ....

10. What talents or accomplishments are you proud of?

✐ ....

11. Name the three people you admire the most. Why do you admire them?

✐ ....

12. What activities do you find most engaging?

✐ ....

12. What issues are you passionate about? What problems do you want to solve?

✐ ....

13. What could you not do? Why not?

✐ ....

14. In which situations do you succeed at what you do naturally and effortlessly?

✐ ....

15. What does success mean to you?

✐ ....

You are now ready to begin the RIASEC questionnaire.

This questionnaire is a powerful tool to discover your personality, and explore your interests, skills, and values. After you've answered the 26 questions, I'll walk you through the RIASEC model. You will understand the different components of your personality in the second part: **Interpreting your RIASEC profile**.

You will then see the occupations related to your profile and select those which attract you the most in the third part: **From RIASEC profiles to occupations**.

I will then show you how to build your career plan and the relevant academic or training path in the fourth part: **Build your career plan**.

Let's go!

PART I

What is your **RIASEC** profile?

How to use the questionnaire

Do this exercise on your own, without outside help, so as not to bias your answers. Plan to keep your answers to yourself. This is between you and yourself. You can choose to communicate only your profile to others.

Answer quickly and as spontaneously as possible. For some questions, you may struggle to answer. If this is the case, pick the closest match or proceed through elimination.

Be authentic, not judgmental. Get rid of any preconceived notion of what your personality should be. There are no good or bad answers, only answers that match YOUR personality.

For this exercise to be useful, you have to free yourself from everything that interferes with your identity, namely:

- Social and family expectations

- Labels you have received since you were born

- Your presumptions about yourself

- The image you want to give of yourself to others

Please take a few minutes to think about what may stop you from accessing your true identity. Now is the time to be yourself!

PRACTICAL ADVICE

- For each question, write down the question number (Q1, Q2, ...) and the letters corresponding to your answers (M, N, ...). This will help you make sure that you don't forget any questions and will let you come back to them if necessary.

- Depending on the question, you will have to select 1, 2, or 4 answers. Read the instructions carefully!

- Form your letters well so that you can count them afterwards.

- At the end of the questionnaire, you will determine your RIASEC profile based on your answers. You will be able to interpret your profile in the next chapter.

Q1: How would you describe yourself?

Choose 4 personality traits.
Write down the 4 letters in your notebook.

P. I am curious about everything.

U. I am frank.

M. I am daring.

O. I am sensitive.

Q. I am athletic.

V. I am studious.

Y. I am optimistic.

W. I am independent.

Z. I am organized.

N. I am cooperative.

L. I am conscientious.

X. I am attentive to others.

Q1: ✎ ___ ___ ___ ___

Q2: What are your primary qualities?

Choose 4 qualities.
Write down the 4 letters in your notebook.

W. I am intuitive.

P. I am logical.

Y. I show initiative.

N. I express myself easily.

Z. I am efficient.

M. I take decisions easily.

X. I am empathetic.

Q. I am practical.

L. I am demanding with myself.

O. I am creative.

V. I am insightful.

U. I am skilled with my hands.

Q2: ✎ ___ ___ ___ ___

Q3: What do you think are your greatest weaknesses?

Choose 4 weaknesses.
Write down the 4 letters in your notebook.

O. Disorganized

Q. Tactless

Y. Reckless

N. Easily influenced

M. Bossy

U. Distant (aloof)

P. Undecided

Z. Rigid

V. Stubborn

X. Idealist

L. Perfectionist

W. Impulsive

Q3: ✎ ___ ___ ___ ___

Q4: What are your guiding values?

Choose 4 values.
Write down the 4 letters in your notebook.

L. Honesty

U. Effort

O. Freedom

V. Knowledge

X. Solidarity

N. Cooperation

Y. Success

W. Beauty

P. Perseverance

M. Power

Z. Order

Q. Common sense

Q4: ✎ ___ ___ ___ ___

Q5: What do you like to do in your spare time?

Choose 4 sentences.
Write down the 4 letters in your notebook.

X. I like to be of service.

Q. I like being in contact with nature.

V. I like to do research on the Internet.

Y. I like to experience strong sensations.

O. I like to go to the movies or see a play.

L. I like to tidy up.

W. I like to write or draw.

U. I like to do manual work.

Z. I like to collect objects, stamps, or photos.

P. I like to read scientific magazines.

N. I like to meet new people.

M. I like to participate in competitions.

Q5: ✐ ___ ___ ___ ___

Q6: When do you feel your best?

Choose 4 possibilities.
Write down the 4 letters in your notebook.

Y. When I have to convince

X. When I work in a team

L. When the organization and the objectives are clear

P. When I try to understand a phenomenon

Z. When I process files or data

V. When I solve a problem

Q. When I use tools or machines

O. When I can express my originality

M. When I undertake projects

U. When I work outdoors

W. When I imagine a new product

N. When I help others progress

Q6: ✐ ___ ___ ___ ___

Q7: What kind of activities do you prefer?

Choose 4 activities.
Write down the 4 letters in your notebook.

V. Intellectual activities

O. Creative activities

Z. Planning activities

X. Activities that are useful to others

L. Filing activities

M. Activities in which I can direct others

Q. Activities that produce concrete results

W. Artistic or design activities

Y. Activities in which I defend my opinion

U. Activities in which I can move

N. Activities aimed at understanding human beings

P. Activities in which I can learn new things

Q7: ✎ ___ ___ ___ ___

Q8: What would you like to do daily?

Choose 4 verbs.
Write down the 4 letters in your notebook.

Q. Build

Y. Negotiate

Z. Check

U. Repair

P. Explore

M. Lead

O. Imagine

N. Explain

L. Work with numbers

W. Create

X. Listen

V. Understand

Q8: ✎ ___ ___ ___ ___

Q9: What do you dislike the most?

Choose 4 sentences.
Write down the 4 letters in your notebook.

P. I don't like negotiating or having to convince someone.

O. I don't like having to follow strict rules.

W. I don't like numbers.

L. I don't like clutter.

Y. I don't like having to think for too long.

Z. I don't like improvisation.

U. I don't like teamwork.

N. I don't like working alone.

M. I don't like science subjects.

Q. I don't like having to express myself in writing.

X. I don't like manual work.

V. I don't like having to lead a team.

Q9: ✐ ___ ___ ___ ___

Q10: What do you absolutely want to find in your occupation?

Choose 4 items.
Write down the 4 letters in your notebook.

X. Human relations

Z. Methods

O. Innovation

V. Science

Q. Physical activity

L. Data processing

Y. Sales

U. Manual work or machine use

N. Opportunities to help others

M. Leadership

W. Creativity

P. Research

Q10: ✎ ___ ___ ___ ___

Q11: What industries appeal to you?

Choose 2 industries.
Write down the 2 letters in your notebook.

V. Computing, Internet or telecoms

N. Social services

U. Agriculture, food, environment

W. Arts and crafts, fashion

P. Research

M. Entrepreneurship

X. Paramedical

Y. Sales and distribution

Z. Administration

O. Audiovisual or entertainment

L. Audit or accounting

Q. Sports

Q11: ✎ ___ ___

Q12: What industries appeal to you? (Bis)

Choose 2 industries.
Write down the 2 letters in your notebook.

Q. Aeronautics, automotive, transportation

V. Biotechnology or chemistry

U. Construction, electronics or mechanics

O. Culture

P. Journalism

M. Marketing

X. Education

L. The army and public security

Z. Banking or insurance

N. Human resources

Y. Politics

W. Graphic design

Q12: ✎ ___ ___

Q13: What would be your ideal work environment?

Choose 4 types of environment.
Write down the 4 letters in your notebook.

U. In front of a machine or behind a steering wheel

Z. A structured and hierarchical environment

V. An intellectually stimulating environment

X. A collaborative open-space environment

W. A colorful and original space

N. A warm and friendly atmosphere

Q. Outdoors and/or in contact with animals

O. A non-conformist environment that fosters creativity

M. A dynamic and competitive environment

L. A safe and comfortable environment

P. A calm environment, conducive to reflection

Y. Where decisions are made

Q13: ✎ ___ ___ ___ ___

Q14: You've become famous. What for?

Choose 2 fields.
Write down the 2 letters in your notebook.

Z. I exposed a health or financial scandal.

W. My invention changed everyday life.

Q. I achieved a sporting feat.

L. I developed new work methods.

N. I organized a large-scale humanitarian action.

U. I received the Technician of the Year award.

X. I revolutionized education.

P. I received the Pulitzer Prize, the highest award for journalism.

O. I created a work of art.

M. I became one of the richest people in my country.

V. I made a major scientific discovery.

Y. I was elected to govern my country.

Q14: ✎ ___ ___

Q15: In your work, it's important that you...

Choose __1__ possibility to complete the sentence.
Write down the letter in your notebook.

Y. ... you can surpass yourself.

N. ... you feel trusted.

V. ... you find meaning.

L. ... your mission is clearly defined.

O. ... you have fun.

U. ... you have the best tools.

Q15: ✐ ___

Q16: What's your primary stress factor?

Choose __1__ possibility to complete the sentence.
Write down the letter in your notebook.

M. Inertia

L. Unexpected demands

O. Rigidity

P. Having to decide quickly

X. Loneliness

U. Relationships

Q16: ✐ ___

Q17: Your career will have been successful if...

*Choose **1** possibility to complete the sentence.*
Write down the letter in your notebook.

X. ... you have made lots of friends at work.

P. ... you have had enriching experiences.

W. ... you have left a mark.

Q. ... you were able to afford a house and a garden.

M. ... you were your own boss.

Z. ... you were recognized for your professionalism.

Q17: ✎ ___

Q18: What do you look for when planning your vacation?

*Choose **1** possibility to complete the sentence.*
Write down the letter in your notebook.

U. Being in nature

P. Learning new things

O. Doing cultural activities

N. Being with friends

Y. Having a sense of adventure

L. Reuniting with family members

Q18: ✎ ___

Q19: What kind of association could you join?

*Choose **1** association.*
Write down the letter in your notebook.

O. A theater company

L. A consumer organization

Y. A political organization

N. A charity

U. A craft workshop

V. A scientific society

Q19: ✎ ___

Q20: What's your favorite word?

*Choose **1** word.*
Write down the letter in your notebook.

Z. Justice

P. Progress

Y. Success

Q. Know-how

O. Dream

X. Peace

Q20: ✎ ___

Q21: You can't stand people who are...

Choose 2 possibilities.
Write down the 2 letters in your notebook.

Q. Hypocrites

N. Antisocial

L. Eccentric

O. Lesson-givers

Y. Indecisive

X. Selfish

Z. Cheaters

U. Nosy

W. Uncultured

P. Loudmouths

M. Nerdy

V. Pretentious

Q21: ✎ ___ ___

Q22: What's your favorite expression?

Choose 2 expressions.
Write down the 2 letters in your notebook.

Q. Practice makes perfect.

O. A picture is worth a thousand words.

Z. Punctuality is the politeness of kings.

N. The more, the merrier.

U. All things come to those who wait.

Y. You're either with me or against me.

W. Better late than never.

P. The pen is mightier than the sword.

L. If you want something done right, do it yourself.

X. Eyes are the window to the soul.

M. Nothing ventured, nothing gained.

V. Knowledge is power.

Q22: ✎ ___ ___

Q23: You're organizing a party with a group of friends. What's your contribution?

Choose 2 possibilities.
Write down the 2 letters in your notebook.

M. You assign tasks and make decisions.

L. You make a budget for the party.

W. You design nice invitations.

Z. You plan the logistics.

N. You phone all the guests.

V. You prepare questions for an escape game.

O. You take care of the decorations and choose the music.

Q. You set up the sound system as well as tables and chairs.

U. You prepare the buffet.

P. You set up a quiet corner.

X. You welcome guests and put people at ease.

Y. You are the life of the party.

Q23: ✐ ___ ___

Q24: You've already received compliments on...

Choose 2 possibilities.
Write down the 2 letters in your notebook.

Z. Your efforts to do well

P. Your good grades

O. Your artistic talents

Y. Your fighting spirit

W. Your originality

X. Your generosity

N. Your kindness

M. Your self-confidence

Q. Your manual skills

U. Your athletic skills

L. Your obedience

V. Your intellectual curiosity

Q24: ✎ ___ ___

Q25: You've already been reprimanded for...

Choose 2 possibilities.
Write down the 2 letters in your notebook.

Q. Your lack of interest in schoolwork

L. Your fussiness

N. Your endless chatter

Y. Your imprudence

V. Your excessive shyness

O. Your hypersensitivity

Z. Your fearfulness

U. Your inability to stay still

X. Your naivety

M. Your insolence

W. Your mess

P. Your never-ending questions

Q25: ✏ ___ ___

Q26: As a child, what was your favorite game?

*Choose **1** game.*
Write down the letter in your notebook.

W. Pictionary™

Z. Card games

M. Monopoly™

X. Hide and seek

Q. Lego™ construction set

P. Scrabble™

Q26: ✎ ___

DETERMINE YOUR RIASEC PROFILE

You've just answered 26 questions and obtained 67 letters. Let's do some math. Don't worry: these are just simple additions!

1. On your notebook, **total each letter and put the number next to the appropriate letter**:

L ___   M ___   N ___

O ___   P ___   Q ___

U ___   V ___   W ___

X ___   Y ___   Z ___

2. Add the letters two by two:

R = Q + U = ___

I = P + V = ___

A = O + W = ___

S = N + X = ___

E = M + Y = ___

C = L + Z = ___

Make sure that the total of the 6 letters is 67.

48

3. Order the totals for each letter from the highest to the lowest and **take the first 3.** For instance, if you got the following results: R=5, I=19, A=12, S=15, E=7, C=9, your RIASEC profile is ISA.

Write down your RIASEC profile:

✐ ___ ___ ___

In addition, you can ask teachers, family, and friends to do the exercise for you. Simply print out or download the simplified questionnaire available on the companion website in the RIASEC questionnaire tab and give it to the people of your choice. To ensure that they answer the questions as freely as possible, tell them to give you only the totals for the letters L, M, N, O, P, Q, U, V, W, X, Y, Z, not the answers. Then calculate the associated RIASEC code. You will thus know how your teachers, family, and friends perceive you!

PART II

Interpret your RIASEC profile

The RIASEC model

John Holland, an American psychologist and career counselor, drew a match between people's personalities and the occupations in which they can succeed and thrive.

His work led him to characterize 6 personality types that together form the RIASEC model:

Realistic

Investigative

Artistic

Social

Enterprising

Conventional.

What is your personality? According to the RIASEC model, your personality encompasses:

- Your interests (what you enjoy doing)
- Your values (what is important to you)
- Your strengths (what you're good at)
- Your weaknesses (what you need to improve)

Research over the past forty years has confirmed the RIASEC model. It shows that a good fit between personality and career choice increases wellbeing and success. The RIASEC model is now used worldwide for career guidance.

Let's be clear from the outset: no type is better than others. Each corresponds to a specific way of functioning that is valuable in the professional environment.

A person's RIASEC profile is established by measuring how similar the person is to each type. It is a three-letter code made up of the initial letters of the top 3 personality types with which the person resonates the most. Thus, an individual characterized by a SER profile would be expected to show traits associated with the Social, Enterprising and Realistic types, in that order.

Just like people can be characterized by 6 personality types, so can work and educational environments. In the RIASEC model, each occupation is assigned a three-letter code, using empirical and judgmental methods to assess the personalities of people who best fit this occupation. It is thus possible to establish for each RIASEC profile a list of occupations that provides a good match for the profile.

The RIASEC model does not offer a magic formula that will reveal THE career for you. But it is a powerful tool to explore your options. Choosing an occupation that correlates well with your interests, values, and skills maximizes your chances of being happy and successful at work.

Note that the RIASEC model allows you not only to better understand yourself but also to better understand others. It will be useful for you later on to work more effectively with your boss, your co-workers, and your subordinates.

Holland's model is represented as a hexagon to show how each type relates to others. The greater the distance between two types, the more different the types are. However, any combination is possible, and all profiles exist.

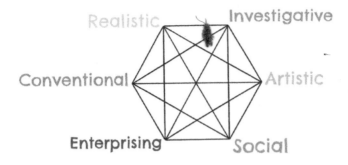

For a given letter, there are 120 possible combinations starting with that letter. Profiles that combine closely related types, such as RIA or IAS, usually choose their careers easily because the three types reinforce each other to form a balanced and identifiable profile. People with profiles that combine distant personality types may find it harder to choose a career. The antagonistic types are Realistic-Social, Investigative-Enterprising, and Artistic-Conventional.

It is possible to accommodate antagonistic types by choosing the right industry. Motivation results from both the nature of the work and the work environment. Let's say your first two letters are C and A, that is to say Conventional and Artistic: you could very well accommodate those two types by choosing a "conventional" occupation in an artistic environment, for instance theater accountant. You can also choose one of the two types for work and use the other in community or leisure activities.

The six personality types

Let's see how we can characterize each personality type so that you can interpret your profile. In the following pages, you will have access to descriptions of each personality type.

Read each description carefully, including the descriptions that do not pertain to your profile, and answer the following question:

For each description, what are the elements that could apply to you? Rank them in order of relevance.

REALISTIC

Manual work, sports & nature

Realistic persons are drawn to hands-on activities and like to use tools or machines.

Of a reserved nature, they prefer to work alone. They tend to remain calm under pressure.

They appreciate tasks with a tangible outcome and a clear purpose. They are wary of abstract concepts. They learn by doing.

They need to move and prioritize action over discussion.

They like animals, plants, and sports. They enjoy spending time outdoors.

Strengths

Calm, common sense, coordination, dependability, dexterity, diligence, endurance, expertise, frankness, patience, practicality, simplicity, technical know-how, tenacity

Areas for improvement

Ability to teach, adaptability, diplomacy, empathy, interpersonal skills, listening, sociability, writing skills

Values

Authenticity, autonomy, competency, durability, experience, hard work, know-how, independence, nature, physical challenge, physical skill, productivity, self-reliance, simplicity, solitude, sustainability, tangible results, temperance, tradition

Favorite activities

Arrange, assemble, build, cook, drive, grow, install, maintain, manufacture, move, produce, renovate, repair, sew

Relevant industries

Aeronautics, agriculture, animal care, catering, construction, crafts, fishing, food preparation, forestry, hotel, maintenance, manufacturing and production, mechanical and electrical engineering, natural resources, space, sports, sustainable development, systems operation, tourism, transportation, urban planning, wildlife

INVESTIGATIVE

Knowledge, science & research

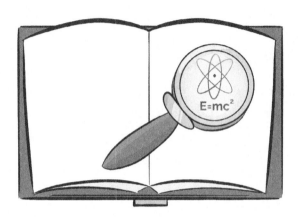

Investigative persons tend to be analytical and scholarly. They are interested in researching, forecasting, solving abstract problems, or studying behaviors.

They are drawn to science, ideas, and concepts. They want to know the why and how. They seek intellectual challenges.

Of a reserved nature, they prefer to work alone in loosely structured environments. They need time to think.

Strengths

Anticipation, capacity for abstraction, capacity for analysis and synthesis, intellectual curiosity, intellectual rigor, logic, open-mindedness, perseverance, tolerance

Areas for improvement

Communication, decision making, leadership, negotiation, persuasive skills, teamwork

Values

Critical thinking, culture, discovery, independence, intellectual growth, knowledge, logic, objectivity, progress, rationality, tolerance

Favorite activities

Analyze, conceptualize, diagnose, experiment, explore, interpret, investigate, learn, probe, read, research, solve, study, understand

Relevant industries

Biology, biotechnology, chemistry, computer science, engineering, human and social sciences, journalism, mathematics, medicine, pharmacy, physics, research

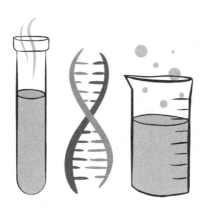

ARTISTIC

Imagination, innovation & emotion

Artistic persons are interested in creative or innovative activities. They need to express their personalities in what they do.

They are drawn to art and literature. They have a vast vocabulary and a deep appreciation for the esthetics.

They seek variety and autonomy. They prefer unstructured activities without strict rules or directives.

They are independent minds that have the ability to think outside the box. They need to be appreciated for their ideas.

Strengths

Adaptability, esthetic sense, autonomy, creativity, design flair, enthusiasm, imagination, intuition, oral and written communication, originality, sensitivity, spontaneity

Areas for improvement

Diplomacy, discipline, organization, perseverance, planning, practicality, time management

Values

Art, beauty, change, freedom, idealism, independence, innovation, inspiration, intensity, originality, passion, spontaneity, variety, vision

Favorite activities

Create, decorate, design, draw, dream, feel, imagine, innovate, invent, paint, play, read, sing, taste, write

Relevant industries

Advertising, esthetics, architecture, arts and crafts, books, broadcasting, cinema, communication, culture, decoration, design, entertainment, fashion, multimedia, music, publishing, theater

SOCIAL

Cooperation, listening & education

Social persons excel at socializing. They are helpful and attentive. They express themselves easily. They are interested in human behaviors.

They are team players. They are friendly but also need to be loved.

They enjoy taking care of children or devoting their time to a cause. They willingly share their time and knowledge with anyone who needs it.

Strengths

Communication, cooperation, dedication, empathy, generosity, kindness, listening, liveliness, patience, positive attitude, responsibility, sociability, team spirit

Areas for improvement

Ability to deal with conflict, assertiveness, frankness, practicality, realism, self-care

Values

Altruism, compassion, consensus, friendship, harmony, kindness, solidarity, trust

Favorite activities

Assist, calm, care, communicate, counsel, educate, entertain, explain, help, inform, interview, listen, protect, rescue, train

Relevant industries

Assistance, communication, counseling, education, entertainment, home care, human resources, humanitarian, leisure, paramedical, psychology, reception, social services, training

ENTERPRISING

Action, negotiation & decision

Enterprising persons seek to influence others and aim for high responsibilities. They want to decide and lead. They excel at persuading, making quick decisions, and carrying out projects. They easily sell ideas or products.

Impulsive by nature, they like challenges and are not afraid to take risks. They appreciate competition. They place great value on power, status, and money.

Energetic and confident, they are often found socializing with others. They have no problems with speaking in public. They need to be seen and like to feel their adrenaline pumping.

Strengths

Assertiveness, audacity, authority, business acumen, charisma, combativeness, decisiveness, determination, dynamism, energy, leadership, optimism, self-confidence, sociability

Areas for improvement

Authenticity, calm, empathy, listening, long-term vision, patience, perseverance, reflection

Values

Action, adventure, ambition, audacity, competition, excitement, fame, materialism, money, performance, power, prestige, risk, speed, status, success

Favorite activities

Be in charge, convince, decide, direct, gain, influence, negotiate, order, organize, sell, succeed, win

Relevant industries

Advertising, banking, commerce, distribution, entrepreneurship, management, marketing, politics, real estate, sales

CONVENTIONAL

Methods, calculus & control

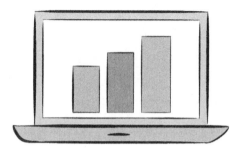

Conventional persons appreciate activities that are clearly defined and that require precision and method. They prefer to work in a structured environment. Office work suits them well. They like to classify or work with data and numbers.

They are respectful of authority and conform to instructions. They have high standards and place great value on reputation. They are thorough in completing work tasks.

They don't like having to improvise and need to be reassured about the quality of their work. They are averse to change and seek job security.

Strengths

Attention to detail, calm, conscientiousness, diligence, discretion, efficiency, loyalty, manners, order, organization, politeness, prudence, punctuality, reliability, responsibility, rigor, self-control, stability, time management, work ethic

Areas for improvement

Adaptability, creativity, imagination, spontaneity, trust

Values

Accuracy, competence, discipline, efficiency, family, honesty, integrity, justice, loyalty, order, precision, predictability, respect, security, stability, tradition

Favorite activities

Administer, budget, calculate, classify, control, count, execute orders, improve, inventory, measure, plan, record, regulate, structure, secure, test, verify

Relevant industries

Accounting, administration, archives, auditing, banking, defense, electronics, finance, information technology, insurance, paralegal, logistics, secretarial work, security, statistics, taxes

Confirm your profile

The previous questions allowed you to determine your dominant type and your two secondary types. Note that you may not have all the characteristics of your dominant type; for instance, you may be Realistic and hate sports.

Take a few minutes to react to the descriptions by answering the 6 following questions:

1. Using the descriptions, score each personality type from 1 to 3. Score 1: this type does not match me at all; score 2: this type matches me a little; score 3: this type is a perfect match.

R: ___; I: ___; A: ___; S: ___; E: ___; C: ___

2. With which personality type do you resonate the most? Give examples of situations that illustrate this.

🖉 ......

3. Which personality types suit you the least? Give some examples.

🖉 ......

4. Do you think the RIASEC profile obtained from the RIASEC questionnaire accurately describes your personality? What surprises you? Why?

 ......

5. Which RIASEC profile do you think would be closest to who you are? Work from your answers to the two first questions.

 ......

6. What did you learn about yourself? Do you want to go deeper into some aspects of your personality?

 ......

You can now correct your RIASEC profile if you think another profile suits you better. This profile will be your starting point in your career choice. You can also work with two or three different profiles: the one obtained from the RIASEC questionnaire, the one you feel is closest to who you are, and the one obtained from family or friends. You are the best judge of your personality, provided, of course, that you are honest with yourself.

Your career must give you the means to express your personality. The classification of professions by RIASEC profiles is based on numerous observations collected in different work environments. It is not intended to deliver an absolute truth but can allow you to explore potential avenues.

Moreover, the same occupation can correspond to different profiles depending on the occupational context, but also on the way one embodies that occupation — for instance, by being practical (R), reflective (I), innovative (A), sociable (S), assertive (E), or rigorous (C). Some occupations can be carried on as a free-lancer (E) or as an employee (S or C, depending on the context).

Therefore, it is important not to limit yourself to the occupations associated with your RIASEC profile, but to explore other combinations by changing the order of the letters or the last letter of your profile. For instance, if your profile is ISA, I invite you to consult the IAS, SIA, SAI, AIS and ASI profiles, and then ISR, ISE, and ISC. A different ordering of the 3 types will be especially relevant if there is not much differentiation among your 3 highest scores.

Write down the 3 letters of your **RIASEC profile:** ___ ___ ___.

Then **the 8 variants** that you will also consult:

Recall the example given earlier: if your profile is ISA, the 8 variants are IAS, SIA, SAI, AIS, ASI, ISR, ISE and ISC.

1. ___ ___ ___

2. ___ ___ ___

3. ___ ___ ___

4. ___ ___ ___

5. ___ ___ ___

6. ___ ___ ___

7. ___ ___ ___

8. ___ ___ ___

Repeat this operation if you have chosen to work with several RIASEC profiles.

WARNING! Nobody fits perfectly to a profile and your personality is not just three letters.

Consider the RIASEC profile as a tool to explore possibilities. It's not a miracle tool. It certainly does not claim to uncover THE perfect occupation for you. Keep in mind that if your RIASEC profile doesn't have all the letters associated with an occupation, it doesn't mean you won't be able to be successful in that occupation. You can find ways to craft most jobs so as to incorporate more of your interests, strengths, and values.

There are many possibilities available to you. Expose yourself to a wide range of occupations before you make a choice.

PART III

From **RIASEC** profiles to occupations

Instructions

1. Locate the first two letters of the profile you want to look at.

2. Go to the page corresponding to the pair of letters.

3. Write down the occupations corresponding to the profile and move on to the next profile.

Profile: ✐ ___ ___ ___

Occupations: ✐ _____

Once you have explored all the profiles that interest you, go to the next chapter.

Recommendation: Assigning RIASEC codes to occupations involves a subjective appreciation of the characteristics of each occupation. For this reason, different sources do not always assign the same codes to the same occupations. It is therefore important not to rely solely on the codes below. In the next chapter, you will understand how to research occupations and assess how they fit your personality.

Realistic Occupations

Keywords:

Outdoors or connection with nature
Manual activities
Use of machines or tools
Construction, manufacturing, repair, or maintenance
Sports
Animal care

REALISTIC INVESTIGATIVE

RI people are drawn to highly technical occupations that combine manual work or physical effort with thinking about the why and how of things. They excel at solving concrete technical problems. They prefer to learn on the job.
Type of activity: autonomous technician.

RIA

Botanist
Eco-designer
Gemstone cutter
Light technician
Naval architect
Oenologist
Photojournalist
Sound technician
Taxidermist

RIS

Hearing care professional
IT and telecommunication technician
Medical radiology technician
Medical technician
Mortician
Veterinarian

RIE

Building craftworker (self-employed)
Dog or cat breeder
Electrician
Horse breeder
Natural heritage project manager

Plumber
Range manager
Refinery operator

RIC

Aerospace engineering and operations technician
Agricultural and food science technician
Automation technician
Automotive service technician and mechanic
Aviation technician
Biology or chemistry technician
Boring machine operator
Cable fitters (wiring specialist)
Civil engineering technician
Clockmaker
Construction equipment operator
Dental prosthesis technician
Electrical and electronics engineering technician
Electrical and electronics installer and repairer
Electrical technician
Electro-mechanical technician
Elevator operator (technician)
Environmental engineering technician
Factory electrician
Flavor technician
Geospatial technician
Industrial engineering technician
Industrial maintenance technician
Installer (alarms, telecoms, solar panels, air-conditioning)
Machine tool operator
Mechanic
Mechanical engineering technician
Meteorological technician

Operator of high-tech machinery
Ornithologist
Pharmacy preparer
Technician in animal experimentation
Telecommunications equipment installer and repairer
Test technician
Veterinary assistant
Wildlife rehabilitator
Wind turbine technician

REALISTIC ARTISTIC

RA people are drawn to manual labor or physical effort associated with innovation, design, or esthetics. They need a lot of leeway. They excel in the concrete realization of products of their imagination. They are "creative technicians".
Type of activity: artisan.

RAI

Acoustical carpenter
Architectural technician
Broadcast technician
Furniture maker
Musical instrument maker
Special effects technician

RAS

Cook
Decorative painter
Graphic arts technician
Make-up artist
Sign maker

RAE

Florist

Head cook

Kitchen or bathroom designer

Leather and shoe worker

Retail store installer

Stunt performer

RAC

Audiovisual technician

Blacksmith

Bronzesmith

Engraver

Farrier

Gardener

Glazier

Ironworker

Landscaper

Lighting designer

Projectionist

Pyrotechnician

Screen printer

Seamstress

Show technician

Stage machinist

Stonecutter

Stonemason

REALISTIC SOCIAL

RS people are drawn to manual work or physical effort that help others. They are "dedicated technicians". This profile is quite rare because it combines two opposite types.

Types of activity: technical assistance, medical technician, sports coach, circular economy, environment.

RSI

Animal behaviorist (ethologist)
Athletic trainer
Environmental consultant
Vocational and technical teacher

RSA

Bartender
Beautician
Hairdresser
Museum technician
Zoo educator
Zootherapist

RSE

Firefighter
Fitness instructor
Mountain guide
Physical education teacher
Taxi driver

RSC

Agricultural consultant
Ambulance driver and attendant
Certified crop advisor

Health assistant
Home assistant
Laboratory technician
Lifeguard
Paramedic
Server
Sports instructor (skiing, horseback riding, swimming, sailing)

REALISTIC ENTERPRISING

RE people are drawn to concrete action and want to be their own boss. They are often self-employed or manage a small team of technicians. They may also be in sales. They are "technical entrepreneurs" or supervisors.

REI

Beekeeper
Breeder
Fish farmer
Fisherman
Harbor pilot
Head of farm operations
Helicopter pilot
Vegetable grower
Wine grower

REA

Caterer
Food craftworker
Horse trainer
Printer
Roofer
Sports broadcaster

RES

Animal seller
Director of natural park
Horticulturist
Pet store manager
Sports coach

REC

Athlete and sport competitor
Captain or pilot of water vessel
Head of general services
Sales agent
Sports event planner
Supervisor in industry
Team leader

REALISTIC CONVENTIONAL

RC people are drawn to manual labor or physical effort for which methods and objectives are clearly defined. They excel in doing precision work and delivering the finishing touch.

RCI

Agricultural inspector
Agricultural worker
Animal caregiver
Arborist
Assembler and fabricator
Auto mechanic
Cartographer
Dental hygienist
Fish farm worker

Forester
Heating engineer
Industrial security technician
Mason
Mechanical drafter
Medical laboratory technician
Orthotist and prosthetist
Plastics technician
Prosthetist
Sports video analyst
Tool and die maker
Topographer
Trail crew member
Waste treatment technician
Water treatment technician
Welder

RCA

3D printing technician
Architectural and civil drafter
Automotive body and glass repairer
Carpenter (wood, metal)
Food manufacturing operator
Furniture restorer
Gemmologist
Kitchen aide
Mirror specialist
Natural or green space maintenance agent
Painter (construction and maintenance)
Pet groomer
Plasterer
Press operator
Tile and marble setter

Upholsterer

RCS

Abattoir operative
Agricultural equipment operator
Airport security officer
Bus driver
Construction worker
Delivery person
Dry cleaner employee
Farm performance operator
Forklift operator
Garbage collector
Hospital cleaner
Industrial technician
Janitor
Locksmith
Mover
Municipal maintenance agent
Nuclear technician
Postal service mail carrier
Prevention and safety officer

RCE

Alligator farmer
Animal control worker
Animal trainer
Cash conveyor
Coast guard
Correctional officer and jailer
Docker
Dog handler
Driller

Forest ranger

Licensed gun dealer

Machine and equipment operator

Minesweeper

Pet store assistant

Professional diver

Rank and file soldier

Referee

Scaffolder

Security guard

Shoemaker

Train or subway conductor

Tree trimmer and pruner

Wildlife enforcement officer

Zoo curator

Investigative Occupations

Keywords:

Reflection and analysis
Scientific research
Problem solving
Social science and humanities
Engineering
Medicine

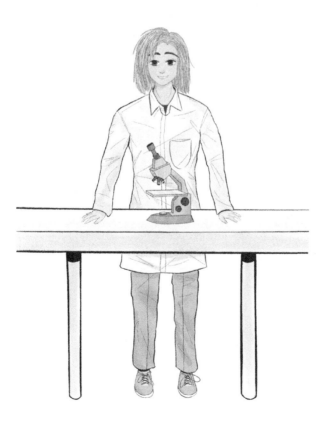

INVESTIGATIVE REALISTIC

IR people are drawn to research or reflection combined with real-world experimentation. They are "researchers in action" or "hands-on scientists".
Types of activity: engineering, experimental research, biology, renewable energy.

IRA

Acoustics engineer
Agricultural and food scientist
Astrophysicist
Automotive engineer
Biologist
Biotechnologist
Chemist
Flavorist
Physicist
Research engineer

IRS

Agricultural engineer
Archeologist
Dentist
Flight instructor
Geologist
Oceanographer
Ophthalmologist
Optometrist
Orthodontist
Paleontologist
Physiotherapist
Private investigator

Radiologist
Seismologist
Sports journalist
Surgeon

IRE

Airline pilot
Forensic pathologist
Forest engineer
Vulcanologist

IRC

Aerospace engineer
Agronomist
Animal scientist
Astronaut
Astronomer
Bioinformatician
Biostatistician
Chemical engineer
Civil engineer
Conservation scientist
Coroner
Environmental engineer
Environmental restoration planner
Environmental scientist and specialist
Food engineer
Geneticist
Geographer
Geospatial information scientist
Greenhouse technician
Hydrologist
Materials engineer

Production engineer
Renewable energy engineer
Soil scientist
Taxonomist
Urban ecologist
Waste management specialist

INVESTIGATIVE ARTISTIC

IA people are drawn to research in order to innovate or create new concepts. They combine logic and intuition. They like to think on their own.
Types of activity: architecture, urban planning, strategy, design, innovation.

IAR

Industrial designer
Product development engineer

IAS

Linguist
Newspaper columnist
Psychometrician
Writer (educational books or personal development)

IAE

Content manager
Copyeditor
Innovation manager
Strategic marketing manager
Strategic planner

IAC

Game designer
Sound engineer
University researcher
Virtual reality designer

INVESTIGATIVE SOCIAL

IS people are drawn to research and inquiries that relate to people, either to study human beings or to be of service to others. Types of activity: medicine, social sciences, humanities, journalism, investigation.

ISR

Biology teacher
Chiropractor
Dermatologist
Engineering teacher
Ethnologist
Gynecologist
Midwife
Osteopathic physician
Physics teacher
Sociologist

ISA

Anthropologist
Criminologist
Economics teacher
Internist
Neuropsychologist
Pediatrician

Philosopher
Psychiatrist
Research professor
Researcher in social sciences (sociology, psychology, history)
Social studies teacher
University professor

ISE

Dietician (freelance)
Forensic psychologist
General practitioner
Political scientist

ISC

Allergist
Audiologist
Corporate journalist
Dietician (health care establishment, collective catering)
Genealogist
Genetic counselor
Historian
Hospital pharmacist
Mathematics teacher
Occupational health physician

INVESTIGATIVE ENTERPRISING

IE people combine reflection and action. They are a rarity. They are drawn to research associated with sales and/or leadership. They are interested in the commercialization of the object of their research or seek to direct their research project.

Types of activity: applied research, marketing, strategy, project manager, sales in the technical and scientific realm.

IER

Pharmacist in the pharmaceutical industry
Real estate operations manager
Technical consultant

IEA

Head of a research laboratory
Market researcher
Political science researcher
R&D project manager
Scientific editor
Solutions architect
Strategy consultant

IES

Emergency doctor
TV or radio reporter

IEC

Clinical research coordinator
Economic developer
Natural sciences manager
Urban planning operations manager

INVESTIGATIVE CONVENTIONAL

IC people are drawn to reflection or research activities within a well-defined framework or in relation to data work.
Types of activity: expertise, computer science, internet, statistics, mathematics, artificial intelligence, forecasting, inspection, law.

ICR

Automation engineer

Back-end developer
BIM manager
Climatologist
Computer hardware engineer
Computer technician
Construction economist
Drone operator
Energy efficiency engineer
Entomologist
Environmental economist
Forensic science technician
Health and safety engineer
Home automation specialist
Industrial IT technician
Mechatronics engineer
Network engineer
Patent scientist
Process engineer
Robotics engineer
Smart city architect
Structural engineer
Technology intelligence analyst
Validation engineer
Weapons system engineer

ICA

App developer
Artificial intelligence engineer
Computer and information research scientist
Computer systems analyst
Cryptographer
Data scientist
Economic analyst

Economist
Front-end developer
Full stack developer
Mathematician
Modeling and simulation engineer
Multimedia designer
Multimedia developer
NLP engineer
Online journalist
Software developer
System architect

ICS

Anesthesiologist
Clinical and epidemiological research engineer
Cognitive scientist
Computer teacher
Computer user support specialist
Demographer
MRI technologist
Pharmacist (in pharmacies)
Scrum master
User experience (UX) designer

ICE

Chief data officer
Computer and information systems manager
Computer network architect
Curator of scientific museums
Ethical hacker
IT consultant
IT project manager
Media planner

Network administrator
Quality engineer
SEO consultant
Strategic intelligence analyst
Survey researcher
Webmaster

Artistic Occupations

Keywords:

Creation
Innovation
Artistic production
Staging

ARTISTIC REALISTIC

AR people are drawn to artistic activities related to manual work, sports, or physical effort. They want to create from concrete material or with their bodies.

Type of activity: arts and craft.

ARI

Color and trim designer
Costume designer
Landscape architect
Painter (artist)
Sculptor
Set and exhibit designer
Theater technician

ARS

Circus artist
Dance teacher
Dancer
Interior designer
Musician
Photographer

ARE

Acrobat
Artisan
Fashion designer
Jeweler
Location manager
Retail merchandiser

ARC

Art conservator
Art technician
Book conservator
Cake designer
Camera operator
Ceramic artist
Glass artist
Goldsmith
Picture framer
Print finishing and binding worker
Prop master
Stained glass artist
Tailor

ARTISTIC INVESTIGATIVE

AI people are drawn to innovative and/or artistic activities combined with research and reflection. They are "intellectual creators".

Type of activity: writing, creation of innovative or creative products, scientific publishing.

AIR

Architect
Automobile designer
Composer
Perfume creator

AIS

Cartoonist
Communications officer

Screenwriter

Sommelier

Writer (fiction)

AIE

Advertising copywriter

Editorial director

Gaffer

AIC

3D animator

3D modeler

Art historian

Digital media designer

Game artist

Graphic designer

Illustrator

Language specialist

Media analyst

Multimedia graphic designer

Multimedia scriptwriter

Orchestrator

Product designer

Sound designer

Sound mixer

Special effects artist and animator

Storyboard artist

Video game designer

Web designer

ARTISTIC SOCIAL

AS people are drawn to artistic activities of service to others. They are "sociable creators".

Types of activity: artistic education, artistic activities, exhibitions.

ASR

Art teacher
Fashion photographer
Music therapist
Singing instructor

ASI

Art therapist
Interpreter
English teacher
Greek or Latin teacher
Foreign language teacher
Music teacher

ASE

Cultural heritage manager
Disk-Jockey (DJ)
Fashion stylist

ASC

Costume attendant
Cultural heritage technician
Internal communications officer

ARTISTIC ENTERPRISING

AE people are drawn to creation associated with marketing or leadership. They are "creative entrepreneurs".

AER

Actor/Actress
Choreographer
Conductor
Food stylist

AEI

Art director
Blogger
Cinematographer
Editor-in-chief
Film or television director
Gallery owner
Music studio owner
Publisher

AES

Booking agent
Casting director
Creative director
Head of advertising
Magazine designer
Music producer
Music publicist
Publishing sales representative
Radio or TV host
Show host
Talent director

AEC

Art auctioneer
Art valuer
Artistic director
Bookseller
Line producer
Music publisher
Producer

ARTISTIC CONVENTIONAL

AC people have both a taste for art and a taste for order and/or precision. They are more rarely found. Reconciling autonomy and security is far from obvious. AC people are drawn to administrative, logistical or control activities around works of art. They are "administrators of the arts" or "meticulous artists".

ACR

Assistant production manager
Book binder
Calligrapher
Piano tuner
Production assistant

ACI

Art critic
Art expert
Desktop publisher
Dialog editor
Film editor
Literary critic
Picture editor

Sound editor

ACS

Assistant curator
Bookstore employee
Librarian

ACE

Art gallery curator
Art museum curator
Cultural heritage curator
Exhibition curator
Film assistant director
Library curator

Social Occupations

Keywords:

Education
Care
Paramedical
Reception
Entertainment
Information and guidance

SOCIAL REALISTIC

SR people seek contact with others though manual or physical activities. They aspire to be of service through concrete achievements.

Types of activity: paramedical, sports, children, training, personal assistance.

SRI

Acupuncturist
Healthcare social worker
Nurse
Nursery nurse
Occupational therapist
Physical therapist assistant
Podiatrist

SRA

Childcare worker
Early childhood educator
Humanitarian technician
Park naturalist
Play therapist

SRE

Community development officer
Humanitarian project manager
Sports retail sales assistant

SRC

Amusement and recreation attendant
Auxiliary-nurse
Childcare assistant

Driving school instructor
Flight attendant
Hotel concierge
Nanny
Retirement community worker

SOCIAL INVESTIGATIVE

SI people seek contact with others in the context of intellectual activities. They aspire to be of service through their reflection. They are advisers.
Types of activity: human resources, personal development, teaching, sociology, psychology.

SIR

Naturopath
Physical therapist
Psychomotor therapist
Sports psychologist
Vocational training instructor

SIA

Educational, guidance, and career counselor and advisor
Image consultant
Kinesiologist
Personal development coach
Psychologist
Self-development coach
Special education teacher
Speech consultant

SIE

Adult educator

Correctional counselor
Health educator
Humanitarian engineer
Policy advisor
Political aide
Social worker

SIC

Human resources analyst
Orthoptist
Psychoanalyst
Recruiting manager
School librarian
Technical support representative

SOCIAL ARTISTIC

SA people seek contact with others in the context of artistic or creative activities. They are "creative sociable".
Types of activity: teaching, communication.

SAR

Activity coordinator
Personal shopper

SAI

Marriage and family therapist
Recreational therapist
School teacher

SAE

Hypnotherapist
Retail sales worker in cultural products

SAC

Training and development specialist

SOCIAL ENTERPRISING

SE people seek contacts with others while leading or managing projects. They are managers or negotiators at the service of others.
Types of activity: community manager, humanitarian work.

SER

Humanitarian developer
Summer camp director

SEI

Head of humanitarian mission

SEA

Family mediator
School principal

SEC

Arbitrator, mediator, and conciliator
Childcare program administrator
Equal opportunity representative and officer
Fundraiser
Human resources manager
Professional matchmaker
Social and community services manager
Trade union official

SOCIAL CONVENTIONAL

SC people seek contacts with others while applying strict guidelines.

Types of activity: reception, public relations.

SCR

Airport stopover agent
Humanitarian mission administrator
Tour guide
Tourist information officer

SCI

Humanitarian logistician
Medical assistant

SCA

Diversity manager
Rehabilitation counselor

SCE

Airline reservation agent
Funeral counselor
Local development officer
Retail salesperson

Enterprising Occupations

Keywords:

Sales
Negotiation
Communication
Management or command
Entrepreneurship
Political activities

ENTERPRISING REALISTIC

ER people are drawn to the management or negotiation of concrete projects. They are "field managers" or "field negotiators".

Types of activity: store manager, sales representative, tourism, hotel industry.

ERI

Fighter pilot
Merchant marine officer
Pharmaceutical sales representative
Ship's commanding officer

ERA

Food store manager
Restaurant manager
Tourism products manager
Wine merchant

ERS

Car dealer
Farm labor contractor
Funeral director
Real estate developer
Service contractor
Sporting goods store manager
Sports agent

ERC

Building contractor
Hotel manager
Plant manager

Real estate broker and sales agent
Small business manager

ENTERPRISING INVESTIGATIVE

EI people who combine reflection and action are a rarity. They are drawn to the management of projects that involve research and reflection. They are "intellectual entrepreneurs ".
Types of activity: marketing, product development, consultancy.

EIR

Broadcast meteorologist
Medical laboratory manager
Optician

EIA

Consultant in innovation management
Green product marketer
Lobbyist
Management consultant
Marketing manager
Sales engineer
Search marketing strategist
Start-up creator

EIS

Bid manager
Career management consultant
Chief of staff
Criminal defense attorney
Headhunter
Human resources consultant
News anchor

EIC

Corporate consultant
Head of sales
Information security manager
Key account sales manager
Trader
Web and mobile product manager
Web marketer

ENTERPRISING ARTISTIC

EA people are drawn to managing or selling artistic or innovative projects. They are "sensitive entrepreneurs".
Types of activity: artistic production, public relations, advertising.

EAR

Merchandiser
Show producer

EAI

Antique dealer
Art dealer
Communications consultant
Director of publication

EAS

Advertising and promotion manager
Advertising sales agent
Artistic agent
Audiovisual programmer
Literary agent
Motivational speaker

Public relations officer

EAC

Advertising media buyer
Advertising media planner
Event manager
Movie or TV producer
Social media manager
Theater director

ENTERPRISING SOCIAL

ES people seek to influence or direct others in order to be of service. They are "leaders in the service of others".
Types of activity: management, consulting, politics, social entrepreneurship.

ESR

Commercial consultant
Fitness and wellness coordinator

ESI

Crisis negotiator
Key account salesperson
Politician

ESA

Announcer
Communications manager
Legislator
Tourist office manager

ESC

Family and divorce lawyer
Hospital manager
Retirement home manager
Training and development manager

ENTERPRISING CONVENTIONAL

EC people like to lead projects that involve the strict enforcement of rules. They are "leaders in the service of law and order".
Types of activity: financial management, security, law, law enforcement.

ECR

Airfield operations specialist
Army officer
Environmental lawyer
Land developer
Police officer
Property manager
Security director
Special forces officer
Store manager

ECI

Broadcast news analyst
Corporate lawyer
Financial services broker
Industrial buyer
Information security officer
Information system administrator
Insurance broker

Police commissioner
Prosecutor
Traffic manager

ECA

Director of private equity investments
Investment director
Investment fund manager
Travel agent

ECS

Administrative services manager
Bank account manager
Bank branch manager
Business unit manager
Care home manager
Community manager
Court administrator
Diplomat
Head of penitentiary establishment
Insurance sales agent
Labor relations specialist
Lodging manager
Medical and health services manager
Purchasing manager
Sales manager

Conventional Occupations

Keywords:

Numbers

Law enforcement

Security

Administration

Office work

Precision work

Logistics

CONVENTIONAL REALISTIC

CR people are drawn to methodical and concrete tasks.
Types of activity: field controller, security, defense, construction.

CRI

CAD technician
Circuit board assembler
City and regional planning aide
Climate change policy analyst
Electrical and electronic controller
Electronic technician
Energy auditor
Environmental auditor
Food safety auditor
Insurance appraiser
Inventory manager
Occupational health and safety technician
Pharmacy technician
Real estate diagnostician
Surveying and mapping technician
Weigher, measurer, checker, and sampler

CRA

Museum guardian
Public works controller
Saddler

CRS

Barista
Dental assistant
Driver's license inspector

Postal service mail sorters, processors, and processing machine operator

CRE

Agricultural grader
Appraiser and assessor of real estate
Bailiff's clerk
Expert surveyor
Freight and cargo inspector
Government property inspector and investigator
Quality control manager
Stock clerk
Transportation security screener

CONVENTIONAL INVESTIGATIVE

CI people are drawn to control activities that require research or reflection.

Types of activity: control, expertise, audit, logistics, insurance, accounting.

CIR

Aviation inspector
Computer numerically controlled tool programmer
Construction and building inspector
Customs and border protection officer
DNA analyst
Examiner, abstractor, and searcher
Insurance expert
Logistician
Non-destructive testing specialist
Occupational health and safety specialist

Real estate expert
Remote sensing technician
Transportation inspector
Transportation planner
Water resource specialist

CIA

Archivist
Artificial intelligence ethicist
Big Data architect
Financial communications officer
Information security analyst
Insurance underwriter
IT security expert
Professional librarian
Risk analyst
Social science research assistant
Software quality assurance analyst and tester
Statistician
Technical translator
Urban and regional planner
Video game tester
Web developer

CIS

Accounting clerk
Actuary
Administrative officer
Auditing clerk
Back-office operator
Billing clerk
Cloud architect
Compensation, benefits, and job analysis specialist

Credit counselor
Data protection officer
Financial quantitative analyst
Judicial law clerk
Law librarian
Payroll manager
Tax preparer

CIE

Administrative law judge, adjudicator, and hearing officer
Air traffic controller
Auditor
Back-office manager
Bank examiner
Claims adjuster, examiner, and investigator
Consolidation manager
Controller
Credit analyst
Credit manager
Database administrator
Financial analyst
Financial auditor
Forensic accountant
Forensic computer analyst
Fraud analyst
Health and safety inspector
Information security auditor
IT security consultant
Labor inspector
Logistics analyst
Quality auditor
Regulatory affairs specialist
Tax examiner and collector, and revenue agent

Treasurer
Yield manager

CONVENTIONAL ARTISTIC

CA people with a taste for both order and art are a rarity. They are drawn to logistics, methods, control, and management activities in relation to arts and innovation.

CAR

Assembly machines conductor
CAD designer
Logistician for the transport of works or art

CAI

Data visualization consultant
Lexicographer
Literary translator
Proofreader
Technical writer
Web and digital interface designer
Web content editor

CAS

Communications assistant
Library assistant
Script

CAE

Certified professional organizer
Publishing secretary
Stage manager

CONVENTIONAL SOCIAL

CS people are drawn to control activities in relation to others. They are "controllers in the service of others".
Types of activity: public service, secretarial work, paralegal.

CSR

Human resources assistant
Postal service clerk
Receptionist and information clerk
Secretary and administrative assistant
Switchboard operator
Travel guide

CSI

General office clerk
Medical secretary
Municipal clerk
Paralegal and legal assistant
Registrar

CSA

Court reporter
Home economics teacher
Tax adviser
Wedding planner

CSE

Ambulance dispatcher
Cashier
Executive assistant
Juvenile justice officer
Legal secretary and administrative assistant

Telephone operator

CONVENTIONAL ENTERPRISING

CE people are drawn to control and management activities while seeking power. They excel in supporting roles.
Types of activity: financial management, asset management, banking.

CER

Bailiff
Cargo and freight agent
Property administrator
Real estate asset manager
Security manager

CEI

Accountant
Business continuity planner
Chief financial officer
Compliance officer
Judge and magistrate
Licensing examiner and inspector
Litigation manager
Tax lawyer

CEA

Investment capital manager
Marketing assistant
Methods manager
Personal finance advisor
Risk manager
Show administrator

CES

Bank teller
Bill and account collector
Brokerage clerk
Family court judge
First-line supervisor of office and administrative support workers
Head of sales administration
Juvenile court judge
Loan officer
Residential advisor

PART FOUR

Build your career plan

1. Explore various career options

In the previous chapter, you identified several occupations that correspond to your RIASEC profile or its eight variants or more if you chose more profiles.

Among all those occupations, choose the 5 that most caught your attention to explore them further:

1. ....

2. ....

3. ....

4. ....

5. ....

Research those 5 occupations.

The objective is to explore each occupation and get as close as possible to its reality. At the end of this research, you should be able to visualize yourself in the occupation. Above all, **be curious!**

To help you in your research, you will find below:

1. How to find information on occupations

2. What questions to ask yourself

HOW TO FIND INFORMATION ON OCCUPATIONS

Consult the Internet. There are ample resources online to explore careers. A list of useful websites is provided at the end of the book. You can also Google search "day in the life of (profession)" and ask questions on Quora, Reddit, or other forums.

Attend Career Days or Job Fairs. You will meet career professionals from various industries willing to share insights on the reality of their careers.

Interview professionals who are already working in that occupation. People usually enjoy sharing their experiences and offering advice. Find people who are located in your geographical area. LinkedIn is an excellent resource to find people.

The questionnaire below will help you prepare a list of questions for the interview. Ask questions that a Google search can't answer. Show that you've done the background search!

Gain exposure to the work setting by work-shadowing someone, volunteering, taking a part-time job, or doing a summer internship in the field that interests you.

QUESTIONNAIRE

To be completed for each occupation

What is the typical career path of someone in that occupation?

Look at education, training, work experiences.

🖉 ....

What is a typical day like?

What are the day-to-day activities? Find action verbs to describe those activities. Can you see yourself doing this for the next 5 to 10 years? What is the activity you would enjoy most? What is the activity you would dislike most? What would be the most challenging?

🖉 ....

What skills and abilities are important to be successful?

Look at requirements in terms of know-how, experience, personality traits, interpersonal skills, and behavioral skills. What kinds of people do well in this career?

🖉 ....

What are the training and educational requirements to secure that occupation?

🖉 ....

In what industries can you find this occupation?

What are the current or upcoming challenges in those industries? In addition, look for examples of companies in which you can find this occupation. Who hires people to do this kind of work?

🖉 ....

What is the typical salary range?

Both for beginners and for people with experience

🖉 ....

What is the outlook for this occupation?

Is this an occupation with good hiring prospects?

🖉 ....

What are the opportunities for advancement and increased responsibilities?

🖉 ....

What are related occupations?

🖉 ....

TAKE THE TIME TO REFLECT

Once you've done the research, answer the following questions for each occupation:

1. Does this occupation correspond to your interests, skills, and values?

✐ ....

2. What draws you to this occupation? What turns you off? Why? *To answer those questions, visualize yourself doing the job.*

✐ ....

3. Among the industries in which you could exercise this occupation, which attracts you the most?

✐ ....

4. Do you feel ready to try for the required qualifications?

✐ ....

2. Choose the right education

MATCH YOUR EDUCATION TO YOUR PROFILE

Below are the most suitable educational and training environments for each personality type.

Realistic

Further education doesn't have to mean a classroom. Favor hands-on learning in vocational or technical programs and apprenticeships. Most of those programs offer a direct path toward specific jobs. You can also look for short-cycle courses.

Investigative

Favor a high-level theoretical education, such as graduate studies.

Artistic

Favor an education that gives you a lot of autonomy and lets you express your creativity.

Social

Avoid competitive environments and prioritize educational environments that emphasize teamwork and the importance of human relations.

Enterprising

Favor competitive environments, such as business schools.

Conventional

Favor structured educational environments, where assessment criteria are clearly established.

The military is a good option if you thrive on structure and physical activity (RC and CR profiles).

Find the right study environment based on your personality and your learning styles. The 10 questions below will help you do that.

A word of advice: **AIM HIGH!**

Motivation is the most effective way to overcome learning difficulties. If you are convinced that you're exactly where you should be, you will give yourself the means to make it happen.

HOW DO YOU VIEW TRAINING AND EDUCATION?

1. What do you like most about training or studying? What do you like less?
Think about what you liked or didn't like about school.

 ....

2. What are the subjects in which you are the most successful? What are the subjects in which you are the least successful?

 ....

3. How long do you want to study for? Do you want to start working as soon as possible?
Consider your personal situation, in particular your financial situation, and your desire to be independent. If you're unsure about study

duration, start small. For instance, a 2-year college may be a great option for now and allows to move to a 4-year school later on.

🖉 ....

4. Do you prefer theoretical studies or more practical training?

🖉 ....

5. What is your academic and psychological profile?
Some courses are more demanding and selective than others. It is better to have a good academic record, to be able to withstand pressure and work long hours.

🖉 ....

EXPLORE SPECIFIC PROGRAMS

Start investigating appropriate education and training programs.

6. How interested are you by the curriculum?

🖉 ....

7. What are the pre-requisites and minimum score requirements? Are they compatible with your academic results?

🖉 ....

8. Do the intensity and total duration of the program suit you?

🖉 ....

9. How much does the program cost? Take into account tuition fees, accommodation costs, cost of living, transportation. How can you finance your way into this program? Are you eligible for financial assistance? Can you find part-time jobs?

Online learning allows to balance a job with an education.

✎ ....

10. Check the quality of the institution. Are the programs accredited by the government? Is the institution recognized as having degree-awarding power? What are the job prospects afterward? What are the alumni doing? How long did it take them to find a job after completing the program?

✎ ....

HOW TO FIND INFORMATION
ON TRAINING AND EDUCATIONAL PROGRAMS

Besides helping you choose an educational or training program, this research will enable you to personalize your applications and prepare for interviews.

Consult the Internet. Visit the program's web page and read about the courses offered and the professors who teach those classes. Look up the rankings. Glean insight from Facebook, Instagram and Tumblr groups devoted to a particular institution or program.

Attend open days to visit the place and ask plenty of questions. You can meet teachers and students and get a glimpse of the academic and social life on campus.

Contact a few alumni. You can reach out to them through LinkedIn, Facebook, or a social media group or look up alumni directories. You can also contact the admissions office: they may have a list of alumni who are willing to talk to prospective student. Don't forget to follow up with an email to say thank you and keep them posted about your decision. Here are a few questions you can ask when applicable:

- Why did you choose this program?

- What did you think of it afterwards?

- What were some of the most defining moments of the program?

- What did you wish the institution did differently?

- What were your favorite classes?

- How did this program prepare you for your career?

- What advice do you have if I attend this program?

Try online courses to audit the subjects that interest you. Coursera, Lynda, and FutureLearn are good resources.

3. Confirm your career plan

Now that you've done all the research, you're ready to make your career choice. It's time to take a few minutes to reflect. You can even let a day go by.

Then make a new selection among the 5 occupations to retain only one. You can do a few iterations if necessary. Begin by ranking the 5 occupations and work on the top 3.

Finally, take a blank page and describe your career plan by copying the following page and completing the sections.

MY CAREER PLAN

Occupation: _____

What I will do daily:

✎ ....

What I like about this occupation (link with my interests and values):

✎ ....

My assets for this occupation (knowledge, strengths, experiences):

✎ ....

The skill I need to develop:

✎ ....

The industries in which I would like to work:

✎ ....

Examples of companies in which I would like to work:

✎ ....

My educational and training project:

✎ ....

The main subjects I will study:

✎ ....

My action plan:

✎ ....

The steps I will take in the immediate future:

✎ ....

YOUR NEXT STEPS

Keep talking with professionals or alumni to get more specific advice on entering your chosen field of work and undertaking your educational and training path.

Share your choices. Use others as sounding boards. Explaining or even defending your choices to those close to you (your friends, your family, your teachers, your guidance counselor) will help you clarify your thoughts and test your convictions. Show how your project is well thought out and how it motivates you.

Look up how to apply for admission to the educational or training program you've identified. Create an excel document to keep track of the deadline/application requirements. Prepare for required entrance exams.

Plan your long-term payment strategy for your education and training. Look for ways to minimize the cost. Apply to scholarships. There are thousands of scholarships that go unclaimed each year. Scholarships are also available for people looking to change their careers.

Conclusion

Choosing is moving forward!

Regarding your career, the final word is yours! You should now have at your disposal your very own career plan. If you need help clarifying certain elements, do not hesitate to consult a professional guidance counselor. And rest assured: a career is not a life sentence! Whatever career path you choose, you can change your mind at any time. Career choice sometimes needs to be done through trial-and-error.

You should revisit your career choices many times over the course of your professional life. You're in a constant process of becoming. As you grow and develop new skills, your interests and values will change; so will your RIASEC profile. Adapt your career plan as you go.

Your career won't necessarily follow a straight path: you won't be doing the same thing all your life, and that's good! You may need to change direction depending on accidents or opportunities along the way. It is estimated that today's young people will occupy an average of 15 different positions throughout their lives with 3 major career changes. The choice you make today is not what you're going to do for the rest of your life, but rather what you're going to try first.

Happiness at work?

When choosing your first job and all the jobs that will follow, you will each time have to define your priorities, in particular with regard to six essential needs:

1. Personal fulfillment (how interesting is the work, is it meaningful? Does it allow you to use your skills and acquire new ones? Do you feel useful?)

2. The level of responsibility

3. The level of income

4. Social status (the prestige of both the position and the company)

5. Quality of life (the balance between private and personal life, commute, working conditions and hours, quality of relationships)

6. Stability (job security, the possibility of a career within the same structure).

Think carefully about what you want to focus on at this time in your life before accepting a position and check that the position allows you to do so. You will then have every opportunity to thrive at work!

I wish you a successful career and hope that this book will have contributed to putting you on the right track.

Before we say goodbye

Thank you for reading this book and walking this path with me. I hope you have found this book enjoyable and useful. Career planning is a subject close to my heart. Gaining readership as an independent author depends mostly on word-of-mouth. If you can, please consider leaving a short review and a rating on Amazon. I look forward to your comments.

Despite my best efforts and many checks, it is possible that some mistakes remain. Thank you for your understanding! For any question or suggestion, do not hesitate to send me an email at contact@whattheheckshouldIdo.com.

See you soon!

Resources

Useful websites and links

Most of the resources below are free although they may require you to set up an account. Some options may come at an additional cost. Please note that a link should not necessarily be construed as an endorsement of all the contents and opinions from the website.

Worldwide

www.careerexplorer.com

Explore careers, jobs, degrees. For each career: overview, salary, job market, how to become, jobs, education, further resources, satisfaction, personality, demographics, work environment. Degrees per area of study. Comprehensive blog: Q&A with professionals, career guides, student advice.

www.thecareerproject.org

Personality and career tests. Career guides (why they actually do, why they are needed, pros and cons, success factors, employability, work environment, career satisfaction, requirements, resources). Job profiles (assessment by a professional based on the concept of informational interviews).

www.glassdoor.com

Millions of jobs searchable by what matters to you. Reviews on over 600,000 companies worldwide from the people that work there. Interview questions to help you prep.

www.topuniversities.com

University rankings: compare top universities from around the world by subject and destination. In-person and online events. Find a course. Career guidance. Study abroad. Scholarships.

www.vault.com

Career Intelligence: find out what it's really like to work within an industry, company, or profession, and how to position yourself to start, advance, or change your career. Company rankings and reviews. Internship programs. Career blog.

www.careers.org

Career advice. Occupation profiles (wages, skills, corresponding college programs). Industry profiles. Online degrees. Detailed profiles for thousands of Colleges and Universities in the United States and abroad, including academic programs, tuition and expenses, and admissions requirements.

www.youtube.com/user/CareerOneStop/featured

Career videos on YouTube

www.jobsmadereal.com

Thousands of career videos. Made by teens for teens.

www.careersoutthere.com

Interviews with professionals.

USA

www.onetonline.org

Occupational Information Network, a national database of occupational interest areas, education and training requirements, earnings, growth projections, and anticipated openings

https://www.bls.gov/ooh/home.htm

Occupational Outlook Handbook. Published by the U.S. Bureau of Labor Statistics. Presents basic career information.

www.candidcareer.com

Thousands of 1-2-minute video interviews with professionals in a wide variety of careers. Insights about their jobs, including the education, training, skills, aptitudes and experience necessary to get hired. Subscription necessary.

www.mynextmove.org

Search career with keywords. Browse careers by industry. Find careers that match your interests and training. Sponsored by the US Department of Labor.

www.apprenticeship.gov

Find the right apprenticeship for you.

www.study.com

Careers and occupations listed by program. Career education programs. Educational requirements. Career summary. Online and campus degrees. Top schools by subject.

career.iresearchnet.com

Career fields and career information.

www.mymajors.com

List of college majors. List of colleges, universities, and career schools. List of careers and job titles. Career pages include description, activities, education requirements, colleges offering related programs, skills, knowledge, work styles, work values, and salary information.

www.studentscholarshipsearch.com

Search, investigate, and apply for scholarships.

UK

www.inputyouth.co.uk

Job guides: the job and what's involved, skills and personal qualities needed, getting started with this career choice, education and training, your long-term prospects, get further information, other related jobs to consider.

www.ucas.com

Universities and Colleges Admissions Service. Study options and qualifications. Apprenticeships and traineeships. Finance and support. Career quiz. Explore job roles (related skills, academic route, essential qualifications, where to find out more).

www.studential.com

Information and advice on all stages of education (GCSEs, apprenticeships, further education, gap years, university, personal statements, postgraduate, US universities).

www.discoveruni.gov.uk

Information and guidance about the different options for studying.

www.thestudentroom.co.uk

Online student community. GCSE, A-levels, applying to uni, university, careers and jobs, student finance.

www.brightknowledge.org

Guide to careers, education, and student life.

nationalcareers.service.gov.uk/ (England)

Learn more about your skills and match them to careers. Explore careers. Find a course.

www.myworldofwork.co.uk (Scotland)

Career advice, job profiles, and tools. Course search, qualifications, and funding. Job search, CVs, and apprenticeships.

www.nidirect.gov.uk/campaigns/careers (Northern Ireland)

Learning and career options. Career discovery tool. A range of interactive tools to help you find out more about your career options, based on your skills, interests and values. Job trends. Career information for key sectors.

careerswales.gov.wales (Wales)

Plan your career, prepare to get a job, and find and apply for the right apprenticeships, courses and training.

Canada

noc.esdc.gc.ca
The National Occupational Classification (NOC) is Canada's national system for describing occupations. You can search the NOC to learn about an occupation: its main duties, educational requirements or other useful information.

www.canadiancareers.com

Career and employment information for Canadians. Explore hundreds of career areas. Learn about market trends. Market yourself. Find work.

www.canada.ca/en/services/benefits/education.html

Student aid and education planning. Find programs and schools. Explore careers. Education requirements by career. Budget your education.

www.jobbank.gc.ca/home

Career planning. Trend analysis. Job search.

www.schoolfinder.com

Explore the career and education options available in Canada. Schools and programs. Scholarships. Events.

umanitoba.ca/careerservices/career-planning/explore-occupations

Explore occupations. Provided by the University of Manitoba.

alis.alberta.ca/occinfo/

Alberta occupational profiles. Discover occupations, jobs, salaries, post-secondary programs, and more.

www.careertipster.com

Career development and education.

www.workbc.ca/blueprintbuilder

Career exploration, education and funding. Job search resources. Save the resources that interest you to your Blueprint.

educationplannerbc.ca/plan

Advice on planning post-secondary education. Application process. Financing. Transition to the workplace.

www.workbc.ca/careercompass

Career quiz. Career listings.

www.talentegg.ca

Jobs. Companies. Career guides. Articles and videos.

Australia

www.yourcareer.gov.au

Resources and information to help you explore all your education, training and work options.

www.joboutlook.gov.au

Information about Australian careers, labor market trends and employment projections.

www.myskills.gov.au

Vocational education and training options, including information about providers, courses, outcomes and fees.

www.myfuture.edu.au

An online career exploration service which includes information on a range of career-related topics.

www.australianapprenticeships.gov.au

Comprehensive information about Australian apprenticeships.

www.mybigtomorrow.com.au

Discover your dream career, experience a day in the life of someone doing that job, and find out how they got there.

http://www.uac.edu.au/

Universities admissions center

Ireland

careersportal.ie

Career advice. Career sectors. World of education (college events, college profiles, course videos, course finder). Student supports. World of work (sector profile, employer profile, career interviews, career videos, career explorer).

www.gradireland.com

Career advice for graduate job hunters.

www.smartfutures.ie

Explore careers in STEM.

www.qualifax.ie

Information about education and training in Ireland.

www.fetchcourses.ie

Information on PLC courses and all courses in the further- and adult-education sectors.

www.apprenticeship.ie

Details of the apprenticeship options

www.whichcollege.ie

Database of courses. Information on career paths and preparation for college.

New Zealand

www.careers.govt.nz

Activities, tools, and resources to make career decisions. Get career ideas and explore study options. Match your school subjects to jobs.

www.justthejob.co.nz

Over 300 career videos arranged under their vocational career pathway headings.

India

www.ncs.gov.in

National Career Service from the Ministry of Labour and Employment. Career information. Videos. Job search. Online job fairs. Career counseling sessions. Career skills program.

www.careerindia.com

Tips and information on courses, exams, scholarships, study-abroad programs, jobs, careers.

www.indiaeducation.net

Information about education at all levels (school education, higher education, continuing education or distance education). Education streams. Entrance exams. Important institutes. Career options. Scholarships. Interviews.

www.careerguide.com/career-options

List of the most popular career options in India. List of institutions in India.

www.mapmytalent.in

Online career counseling website. A battery of assessments specifically designed for Indian careers. Career test packages.

www.shiksha.com

Information for students interested in undergraduate and postgraduate courses in India and abroad. Career test packages.

www.careerizma.com

Free career resources. Guide to career options in India (occupations, salaries, career path, qualifications). List of industries and key skills. Online career counseling packages.

www.mindler.com

Career counseling and college application programs.

Printed in Great Britain
by Amazon